This book is dedicated to Rosie. "Sing the song that's in your heart, and dance until you die."

Edited by Aileen Andres Sox
Designed by Dennis Ferree
Art by Kim Justinen
Typeset in 14/18 Weiss

ISBN: 0-8163-1182-X

94 95 96 97 98 • 5 4 3 2 1

Red and Purple on My Feet

By Linda Porter Carlyle   Illustrated by Kim Justinen

Pacific Press Publishing Association
Boise, Idaho
Oshawa, Ontario, Canada

e are hurrying down the highway. I am watching for baby animals. I have seen seventeen lambs and twelve baby cows and one mother hen with chicks. "Oh, no!" Papa says. The car slows down, and Papa pulls over to the side of the road.

"What's the matter, Papa?"

 look around. There is a police car behind us with a big, bright, flashing red light on the roof. The police officer comes to Papa's window. "May I see your license, sir?" she asks.

"What's the matter, Papa?"

"Sh!" Papa says.

hen the police officer is finished talking to Papa, she goes back to her car. Papa looks at the piece of paper the officer gave him. He looks at me. "I made a bad choice," Papa says. "I decided to go over the speed limit. I was driving too fast, and now I have to pay a fine."

"What's a fine, Papa?"

 am ready for breakfast. I dance through the kitchen door. "I'm hungry, Mama!"

Mama looks at me. "My, aren't you colorful today!" she exclaims. I turn around carefully so she can see my whole outfit. I think I look elegant. I pick up my feet, one at a time, so she will see my socks too. I am wearing one red one and one purple one.

o you want cold cereal or hot cereal for breakfast?" Mama asks.

"I want hot oatmeal with peanut butter and maple syrup on the top," I say.

"OK," Mama answers. "I'll call you when it's ready."

Do you want to taste my cereal?" I ask Mama.

"Sure," Mama says. She takes a little bite and smiles. "Not a bad choice," she says.

You know," Mama continues, "life is full of choices. We have so many choices to make each day that we probably couldn't even count them all."

ike my clothes," I say. "I chose everything I'm wearing today all by myself."

Mama chuckles. "Like your clothes," she says. She takes another bite of my cereal. "Some of our choices are little choices," she says. "It doesn't really matter what we decide. Like your breakfast. Hot cereal and cold cereal are both good for you. It didn't matter which one you chose. But some choices are big and very important. Can you think what might be a big and important choice?"

I stop chewing. I look out the window. I am thinking. "Not to take Katie's new red rubber ball and keep it," I say. I sigh. Katie's new ball is the bounciest ball I have ever played with.

Mama smiles at me. "That's right," she says. "It's an important choice not to take something that doesn't belong to you."

 smile back at Mama and then scrape the last bit of peanut butter out of my bowl. "Jesus helps me make good choices," I say.

Mama looks surprised.

"Well, you told me that He does, and I remember," I say.

Mama looks pleased. "I'm so proud of you!" she says. "As long as you ask Jesus every day to help you make good choices, you'll do very well!"

 know," I say. I slide off my chair. I pick up my bowl and spoon. "Look, Mama, I am choosing to take my dirty dishes out to the kitchen."

Mama laughs. I laugh. Good choices make me happy.

 can choose to be good even if it's hard.

I can pray, "Jesus, help me always be like You."

Parent's Guide

Help Your Child Learn to Make Good Choices

It is every parent's desire to have our children grow into truly responsible adults. In order to do this, children need to learn to make good choices. It is hard to watch our children make poor choices, but if we try to make all their little decisions for them, there is no way that they will be prepared when it comes to making the major decisions only they can make.

❖ Give your child two options (both of which would be acceptable), and let her choose. "Do you want to wear your blue shirt or your yellow shirt today?" "Would you rather take your bath before or after story time?"

❖ Resolve to make your home a place in which it is OK to fail. Try to use a bad choice as a teaching tool instead of a reason to berate. We want to let our children learn from the poor choices they might make. One little girl we know wore her church shoes outside to play without permission. When she came in the house again, the shoes were badly scratched. "Mommy, you fix them," she said. Mommy had to reply, "I can't fix them. You chose to wear them for play. You can see that wasn't a good idea!"

❖ Let your child share the process you go through in making decisions. For example, you could let him help you plan the evening meals for a week. You can talk about the kinds of food that should be eaten at each meal. And when he is old enough, you can add the component of price into the decision-making process.

❖ Remember that not all choices are life-and-death ones. Many of them involve personal preference more than moral matters. In this book, Danielle's mother respected her and her choice of clothing for the day. It was not immodest or inappropriate for the weather. It was an expression of her individuality and creativity. Our children's self-esteem will grow when we respect their decisions. Of course, we will want to influence their taste, but we can do it subtly, rather than in a domineering manner.

❖ Remember that God gives us freedom of choice. As sin has proven, this was a risky thing for God to do. It is also risky for parents. But if we empower our children to make good choices and give them a loving Christian example, one day we will hear them say, as did Joshua, "As for me and my household, we will serve the Lord" (Joshua 24:15, NIV).

Linda Porter Carlyle and Aileen Andres Sox

Books by Linda Porter Carlyle

I Can Choose
A Child's Steps to Jesus

God and Joseph and Me	*No Olives Tonight!*
Rescued From the River!	*Happy Birthday Tomorrow to Me!*
Grandma Stepped on Fred!	*No Puppy Food in the Garden*
Max Moves In	*Red and Purple on My Feet*
Cookies in the Mailbox	*Teddy's Terrible Tangle*
Beautiful Bones and Butterflies	*My Very, Very Best Friend*